A Morning with Grandpa

Sylvia Liu

illustrations by Christina Forshay

Lee & Low Books Inc. | New York

Gong Gong (goong goong): Grandfather, Grandpa

Mei Mei (may may): little sister

qi (chee): Chinese word for "energy" or "life force"

tai chi (tahy jee): Chinese martial art and exercise

yoga (yoh-guh): Indian form of meditation and exercise

Thank you to Ed Young, tai chi master, and Kimi Weart and Sandy Florian, yoga practitioners,
for reviewing the movements and poses in the illustrations.

Book design by Kimi Weart
Book production by The Kids at Our House
The text is set in Neucha
The illustrations are rendered digitally
Manufactured in China by Jade Productions, April 2016
Printed on paper from responsible sources
10 9 8 7 6 5 4 3 2 1
First Edition

Library of Congress Cataloging-in-Publication Data
Liu, Sylvia, author.
A morning with grandpa / Sylvia Liu ; illustrations by Christina Forshay. —First edition.
pages cm
Summary: Curious and energetic Mei Mei attempts some t'ai chi forms as her grandfather demonstrates them,
then tries to teach him basic yoga poses. Includes introductions to t'ai chi and yoga, as well as instructions for the
exercises described in the text. Includes bibliographical references.
ISBN 978-1-62014-192-2 (hardcover : alk. paper)
[1. Tai chi—Fiction. 2. Yoga—Fiction. 3. Grandfathers—Fiction.] I. Forshay, Christina, illustrator. II. Title.
PZ7.1.L585Mor 2016 [E]—dc23 2015018278

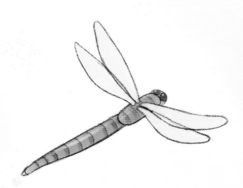

Mei Mei watched Grandpa dance slowly among the flowers in the garden. He moved like a giant bird stalking through a marsh. His arms swayed like reeds in the wind.

"What are you doing, Gong Gong?" asked Mei Mei.

"I am practicing tai chi," said Gong Gong. "This form is called White Crane Spreading Its Wings."

"What's tai chi?" asked Mei Mei.

"Tai chi is a martial art that sends good energy through your body. The energy is called *qi*," explained Gong Gong.

"Martial art!" said Mei Mei, bouncing up and down.

"I can do karate. HI-YAH!"

"Tai chi isn't that kind of martial art," said Gong Gong. "I will teach you. This is Pick Up the Needle from the Sea Bottom."

In one smooth motion, Gong Gong stepped back, bent over, and swept one arm low. He moved like seaweed brushing the ocean floor.

"Now you try," said Gong Gong.

Mei Mei stepped back like a young frog trying out new legs. She hopped and bopped and bumped into Grandpa.

"How was that, Gong Gong?" asked Mei Mei.

"Not quite right," Gong Gong replied. "Try to move more slowly and breathe in deeply. Then breathe out."

"Let's try something else," said Gong Gong. "This is called Cloud Hands."

Gong Gong stepped from side to side and carefully moved his arms back and forth. He was a warm summer breeze gently blowing through the trees.

Mei Mei was a frisky fall wind tumbling among the leaves.

"Slow down," said Gong Gong. "Use your breath to move the energy around your body."

"Energy moves around my body all by itself," said Mei Mei.

Mei Mei **twirled** like a helicopter seed flying down from a maple tree.

"Very nice, Mei Mei," said Gong Gong. "Now let's try Play the Lute."

Gong Gong rocked backward and then forward. One arm went up while the other came down. He was a musician serenading the sunflowers.

Mei Mei was a **rock star** playing guitar for the daisies.

Gong Gong conducted
a quiet symphony.

Mei Mei **drummed**
the earth with hands and feet.

"How am I doing, Gong Gong?"

"Perfect, Mei Mei."

"Now that I'm really good at tai chi, it's my turn to teach you something new," said Mei Mei. "We learned how to do yoga in school."

"Yoga! That's very hard, isn't it?" asked Gong Gong.

"It's not hard, Gong Gong. Yoga makes you strong," said Mei Mei, flexing her muscles.

"Just copy me," said Mei Mei. "Let's do Downward Dog. *WOOF, WOOF!*"

Mei Mei planted her hands and feet on the ground and shaped her body into an upside-down letter *V*. She stood like a guard dog, strong and steady.

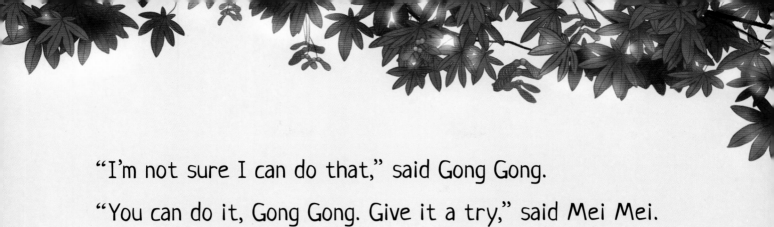

"I'm not sure I can do that," said Gong Gong.

"You can do it, Gong Gong. Give it a try," said Mei Mei.

Gong Gong tried to bend into a V shape too. He wobbled like an old dog, creaky at the knees.

"Now let's try the Cat," said Mei Mei, getting on her hands and knees. She arched her back like a kitten ready to play.

"This looks easier. I will give it a try," said Gong Gong.

On his hands and knees, Gong Gong hunched his back to the sky. "Me-*OWWWW*," he yowled like a startled cat.

"How about we try the Mermaid?" Mei Mei asked.

She sat with one leg bent behind her and the other leg folded in front. One hand rested on her back foot, and the other hand lifted to the sky.

Mei Mei was a creature of the deep sea guarding treasures.

"Are you sure it's not called the Pretzel?" asked Gong Gong. "That looks complicated."

"Try it," said Mei Mei.

Gong Gong twisted his leg this way and that, and almost fell over. He was a fish in the water trying to escape a dangling hook.

"I'm not made for the sea," said Gong Gong.

Mei Mei helped her grandpa to his feet.

"Gong Gong, I know you can do yoga," said Mei Mei. "Let me think. Oh! I know. Can you be a Tree?"

"A tree? I love trees," said Gong Gong.

"Me too," said Mei Mei. "They're the best. Let's be trees."

Mei Mei lifted her leg and *stretched* her arms like branches reaching high to the sky. Her tree wobbled and bent to one side.

Grandpa slid his leg up and raised his branches too. His tree leaned the other way.

Mei Mei and Gong Gong were two royal palms swaying in the wind.

"How did I do, Mei Mei?"

"Perfect, Gong Gong."

TAI CHI

Tai chi is short for Tai chi chuan, which means "ultimate supreme boxing" in Chinese. Tai chi is a popular type of exercise that is also considered a martial art. When doing tai chi, people move slowly, breathe deeply, and direct their *qi*, or energy, around their bodies. They go through a series of connected movements, called forms. Tai chi helps people stay healthy and flexible.

The most common style of tai chi includes twenty-four forms. In this story, the tai chi forms are not performed in their usual order.

White Crane Spreading Its Wings: Take a small step with your right leg and then lift your left leg up and bring it lightly down in front of you. At the same time, circle your right arm above your head and sweep your left arm low to your thigh as if you are about to do a grand bow.

Pick Up the Needle from the Sea Bottom: With your left leg slightly bent in front of you and your right leg slightly bent behind you, step up and reach down. End in a half crouch, with your left foot pointed forward, your weight on the back right leg, and your right arm sweeping low.

Cloud Hands: While moving from side to side, shift your weight from one leg to the other and pretend to pass a beach ball back and forth. Each time, switch the top and bottom hands.

Play the Lute: Step with your right foot, rock backward and then forward while stretching your left arm up and bringing your right arm down as if playing a stringed instrument. End with your left foot pointing up.

YOGA

The term "yoga" comes from the Sanskrit word that means "union." Yoga is an ancient mind and body practice from India that focuses on balance and inner peace. There are many different types of yoga. People who practice yoga do postures called "asanas." Performing the postures helps people become strong and flexible. Yoga also focuses on the union between asanas and breath.

The asanas in this story are as follows.

Downward Dog: With your hands and feet on the ground, lift your hips to the sky and turn your body into the shape of an upside-down letter V.

Cat: With your hands and knees on the ground, slowly arch your back and let your head drop to your belly.

Mermaid: This is an advanced pose but can be modified for beginners. Start by sitting on the ground. Bend your left leg in front and bend your right leg behind you. Place your right hand on your right ankle. Inhale, and reach your left hand toward the sky. The advanced version starts the same, but the right leg is stretched out behind you. Lift your right foot up to rest inside the crease of your right elbow. Link your hands and hold them behind your head.

Tree: Stand with both feet together, then balance on one leg. Bend your other knee and draw your foot to the thigh or calf of your supporting leg. Hold your hands together at your chest or extend your arms above your head.

AUTHOR'S SOURCES

Garofalo, Michael P., researcher. "List of Movements: National Standard T'ai Chi Ch'uan 24 Short Form." Valley Spirit Taijiquan. http://www.egreenway.com/taichichuan/short.htm#List.

Iknoian, Therese. *T'ai Chi for Dummies*. New York: Wiley Publishing, 2001.

Lee, Cyndi. "Yoga 101: A Beginner's Guide to Practice, Meditation, and the Sutras." *Yoga Journal*, October 7, 2014. http://www.yogajournal.com/article/beginners/yoga-questions-answered/.

Luby, Thia. *Yoga for Teens: How to Improve Your Fitness, Confidence, Appearance, and Health—and Have Fun Doing It*. Santa Fe, NM: Clear Light Publishers, 2000.

Man-ch'ing, Cheng. *T'ai Chi Ch'uan: A Simplified Method of Calisthenics for Health & Self Defense*. Berkeley, CA: North Atlantic Books, 1981.

Martin, Robert C. "Tai Chi 24 Form, with English Titles." YouTube video, April 14, 2008. https://www.youtube.com/watch?v=-ZtpwmjMC7Q.

"Mermaid Pose." Namaste Kid. http://www.namastekid.com/learn/kids-yoga-poses/mermaid-pose/.

Pawlett, Ray. *The Beginner's Guide to Tai Chi*. New York: Sterling Publishing Co., 2001.